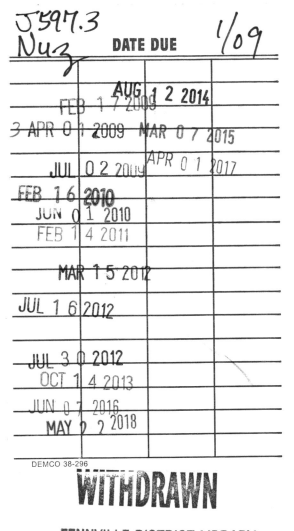

J 597.3
Nuz

DATE DUE 1/09

	AUG 1 2 2014	
FEB 1 7 2009		
3 APR 0 1 2009	MAR 0 7 2015	
JUL 0 2 2009	APR 0 1 2017	
FEB 1 6 2010		
JUN 0 1 2010		
FEB 1 4 2011		
MAR 1 5 2012		
JUL 1 6 2012		
JUL 3 0 2012		
OCT 1 4 2013		
JUN 0 7 2016		
MAY 2 2 2018		

DEMCO 38-296

Sharks

Tiger Shark

by Deborah Nuzzolo

Consulting Editor: Gail Saunders-Smith, PhD

Consultant: Jody Rake, member
Southwest Marine/Aquatic Educators' Association

Capstone
press

Mankato, Minnesota

Pebble Plus is published by Capstone Press,
151 Good Counsel Drive, P.O. Box 669, Mankato, Minnesota 56002.
www.capstonepress.com

1 2 3 4 5 6 13 12 11 10 09 08

Library of Congress Cataloging-in-Publication Data
Nuzzolo, Deborah.
    Tiger shark / by Deborah Nuzzolo.
       p. cm. — (Pebble plus. Sharks)
    Includes bibliographical references and index.
    Summary: "Simple text and photographs present tiger sharks, their body parts,
and their behavior" — Provided by publisher.
    ISBN-13: 978-1-4296-1730-7 (hardcover)
    ISBN-10: 1-4296-1730-6 (hardcover)
    1. Tiger shark — Juvenile literature. I. Title.
QL638.95.C3N89 2009
597.3'4 — dc22   2007051337

Editorial Credits
Megan Peterson, editor; Ted Williams, set designer; Kyle Grenz, book designer; Jo Miller, photo researcher

Photo Credits
Getty Images Inc./National Geographic/Bill Curtsinger, 20–21; National Geographic/Brian J. Skerry, 19;
    Science Faction/Stuart Westmorland, 10–11
iStockphoto/Chris Dascher, 1
Nature Picture Library/Jeff Rotman, 4–5
Peter Arnold/Franco Banfi, 17; Hanson Carroll, 13; Jonathan Bird, 14–15; P. Ryan, 7
Seapics/Andre Seale, 9
Shutterstock/Simone Conti, backgrounds
SuperStock, Inc./Pacific Stock, cover

Note to Parents and Teachers

The Sharks set supports national science standards related to the characteristics and
behavior of animals. This book describes and illustrates tiger sharks. The images support
early readers in understanding the text. The repetition of words and phrases helps early
readers learn new words. This book also introduces early readers to subject-specific
vocabulary words, which are defined in the Glossary section. Early readers may need
assistance to read some words and to use the Table of Contents, Glossary, Read More,
Internet Sites, and Index sections of the book.

Table of Contents

Striped Sharks

How did tiger sharks

get their name?

They have stripes like a tiger.

Tiger sharks spend the day
in deep water.
At night they swim into warm,
shallow water to hunt.

Tiger Shark Pups

Between 10 and 80
tiger shark pups
are born at one time.
They live and grow
on their own.

tiger shark pup

A tiger shark's spots and stripes

fade as it grows.

Some adults don't have stripes.

What They Look Like

Tiger sharks have
sharp, rounded teeth.
They can cut open
a sea turtle's shell.

14 feet (4.3 meters) long

5 feet (1.5 meters) long

Tiger sharks have gills
on each side of their head.
Sharks use their gills
to breathe underwater.

gills

Hunting

Tiger sharks hunt fish,

sea snakes, seals, and squid.

They also hunt other sharks.

Tiger sharks eat
whatever they find.
They even eat garbage
like cans and bottles.

Tiger sharks are
dangerous hunters.
They will eat anything
in the sea.

Glossary

dangerous — not safe

fade — to become paler in color

gill — a body part that a fish uses to breathe; gills are the slits on the sides of a shark's head.

hunt — to chase and kill animals for food

pup — a young shark

shallow — not deep

Read More

Crossingham, John, and Bobbie Kalman. *The Life Cycle of a Shark.* The Life Cycle Series. New York: Crabtree, 2006.

Lindeen, Carol K. *Sharks.* Under the Sea. Mankato, Minn.: Capstone Press, 2005.

Simon, Seymour. *Sharks.* New York: Collins, 2006.

Internet Sites

FactHound offers a safe, fun way to find Internet sites related to this book. All of the sites on FactHound have been researched by our staff.

Here's how:

1. Visit *www.facthound.com*

2. Choose your grade level.

3. Type in this book ID **1429617306** for age-appropriate sites. You may also browse subjects by clicking on letters, or by clicking on pictures and words.

4. Click on the **Fetch It** button.

FactHound will fetch the best sites for you!

Index

Word Count: 136

Grade: 1

Early-Intervention Level: 18

24